UNSTUCK

UNSTUCK

100 Journal Prompts to Break the Rut

BRIAN LEAF

Skyhorse Publishing

Skyhorse Publishing books may be purchased in bulk at special discounts for sales promotion, corporate gifts, fund-raising, or educational purposes. Special editions can also be created to specifications. For details, contact the Special Sales Department, Skyhorse Publishing, 307 West 36th Street, 11th Floor, New York, NY 10018 or info@skyhorsepublishing.com.

10 9 8 7 6 5 4 3

Library of Congress Cataloging-in-Publication Data is available on file.

Cover design by Laura Klynstra
Cover illustration by gettyimages

Print ISBN: 978-1-5107-4589-6
Ebook ISBN: 978-1-5107-4590-2

Printed in China

To Swami Kripalu

Table of Contents

How to Use This Book

It's time to break the rut. Maybe you want to inject fresh energy into your work life, home life, romantic relationship, or spiritual life. Maybe you are an artist and need a creative boost. Maybe you have always dreamed of being an artist and it's time to take the leap. Or maybe you just feel a bit unsatisfied, unmotivated, unchallenged, and frankly, stuck.

Well, this journal is here to help you get *un*stuck!

There's no wrong way to use this book. You can start at the beginning and work your way through, page by page. You can start with one of the categories (body, mind, heart, or spirit), you can work backward from the last page to the first, you can leave it to chance and flip open to a random page, or, my favorite, you can call upon God or your angels to guide you to exactly the page you need today.

I.

Body

Small changes
to your daily habits,
exercise routines,
and diet
can have a
profound
effect
on your energy level,
motivation,
endurance,
and creativity.

These prompts are especially useful
if you are feeling
stiff, lethargic, or foggy.

Put down this book for a few moments and breathe deeply while smiling.

Set a reminder on your smartphone to do this every two hours. Watch for flashes of creativity.

Every time you feel blocked or stuck today, drop whatever you are doing and do some vigorous exercise, if even just twenty-five jumping jacks or a brisk walk up and down the block near your home or office.

Give up refined sugar (candy, white sugar, desserts, Twinkies) for three days starting now. You can do it! I believe in you! Watch for any changes in your energy level, mood, or creativity.

Record results at the end of each day.

Day 1: ______________________________

Day 2: ______________________________

Day 3: ______________________________

Yoga Break

Lie on your back with knees bent, feet flat on the floor. Squeeze this book between your knees. Try to keep it squeezed as you slowly, mindfully raise and lower your pelvis. Feel what muscles are working hard and what muscles are being stretched. Feel your spine raising and lowering one vertebra at a time.

Choose a place in which you feel stuck in some way. Maybe at your desk, on your commute to work, in the kitchen, near your dresser, or in bed. Make a shift to be in that place from a new angle. Turn your desk, switch sides of the bed, take a new route to work, chop veggies in a new area of the counter. Anything to see from a new angle.

Shake up your status quo. At every opportunity today, when possible, make a different choice than you usually do. Dress a bit differently. Park in a different spot at work. Have a different lunch. Say hello or goodbye in a different way. If you are a hugger, then wave, or vice versa.

Sitting wherever you are right now, as you read this page, practice a simple body scan relaxation:

1. Bring your awareness into your feet and legs. Feel your clothing or the air touch your legs. Consciously relax the muscles in your feet and legs.
2. Bring your awareness into your hips and pelvis. Notice the sensations in your hips and pelvis as you sit here right now. Consciously relax and soften the muscles in your hips and pelvis.
3. Bring your awareness into your belly, chest, and back. Breathe deeply. Consciously relax all the muscles in your belly, chest, and back.

4. Bring your awareness into your neck and shoulders. Stretch to release tension. Consciously relax all of these muscles.
5. Bring your awareness into your face and scalp. Breathe out with a sigh as you release tension in your face and scalp.
6. Now, allow yourself to inhabit all of your body: feet, legs, pelvis, belly, back, chest, shoulders, neck, face, and scalp. Breathe. Relax all of these areas a little more.

See if you can bring this embodied, relaxed experience into the rest of your day.

Two words: Oil Pulling. This is the natural health practice of swishing organic coconut oil around your mouth for ten minutes each morning before eating. Try it for the next five days. Take a few notes below after each swish session. (Note: After the ten minutes, you have to spit the oil into the trash, not the sink, so it doesn't clog the plumbing.)

Day 1: ______________________________

Day 2: ______________________________

Day 3: ______________________________

Day 4: ______________________________

Day 5: ______________________________

Choose a day sometime this month when you're not in too much demand, and between breakfast and dinner, don't eat. Drink only water. Have a light, healthy dinner and no snacks before bed. The next day, you may feel energized and renewed. Describe your experiences below.

Try more sleep this week. Go to bed earlier, sleep in longer, make time for a nap. Your productivity and mood will likely improve. Record results below.

Chose a cluttered corner of your bedroom or office and clear it out today. Make it tidy and clean. Afterward, sit for a few moments and feel the clarity. Describe it below.

Try a bit more or a bit less caffeine today. How does this affect you? Record your feelings below.

Do gentle simple stretches for five minutes every morning and every night this week. You don't have to be a yoga master to do this, just experiment and find any stretches that feel good. Breathe and relax and moan or sigh as you stretch and release muscle tightness. You can do this in your bedroom, on a yoga mat, or even simply in bed under the covers. Notice how you feel afterward and notice how stretching your body wakens your mind.

List your four favorite quick and simple ways to have fun.

1. ______________________________

2. ______________________________

3. ______________________________

4. ______________________________

Do them all at some point this month. Open your planner and program them into your schedule.

Get some sun today. Sit in the park at lunchtime or go for a walk. Soak up the sun on your face.

Choose one:

- ☐ Breathe deeper today, all day, especially outdoors. Savor the fresh air. Set a reminder on your phone.
- ☐ No elevators this week. Take the stairs.
- ☐ For the next three evenings, don't snack after dinner. Watch how much more energy you have in the mornings.

Add some spice to your diet today. Literally. Try ginger, garlic, chili flakes, black pepper, cumin, coriander, oregano, or basil. Notice if it aids your digestion, improves your mental clarity, and increases your energy level. Experiment with different spices this week and keep notes below.

Get outside in the evening every day this week. Soak in the moonlight. Look at the stars. Find the Big Dipper. Notice the magical feeling of evening and nighttime.

Next rainy day, go outside and get soaked. Totally drenched.

(Just make sure you've got a warm bath or shower waiting for you.)

Go today to a local
bookstore or library
and pick out a book
to read. Spend time
every evening this week
reading your new book.

Try something new and even a little bit risky in your work, home life, or relationship today. Make a plan below:

Today I am going to . . . ______________________________

____

____

____

____

____

____

____

____

Close the blinds and dance naked.

Tear out this page violently,
like a frustrated writer.
Crumple it up and toss it into
the recycling bin. Then get to
work fresh on the next page.

II.

Mind

Change
the way
you
see
yourself
and
the way
the world
sees
you
will change.

These prompts
help you free
your mind,
see things in a new way,
and
open yourself to new possibilities.

Collaborate today on something you would usually do alone. Let someone in.

Record results below.

For the rest of today, at the top of every hour, stop what you're doing, feel your feet on the ground, look around, take in your surroundings, and mindfully say "Here I am."

Set an hourly reminder on your phone so you'll remember.

Spend a half day this weekend in nature. Take a hike, canoe ride, bike ride, or just a stroll. Notice the trees and flowers and bugs and birds. Sketch a few in the space below.

Follow none of your usual routines this week. Do new things at new times and see different places.

Choose a very simple object that you interact with regularly, such as a pencil, mug, or eyeglass case. Hold it, turn it around in your hands, and see with fresh eyes, as though for the first time. Notice subtle aspects of it. Experience it as it is right now. Describe its every detail below.

In the space below, copy the first few lines of a favorite scene from your favorite book or movie. Then, create some fan fiction. Give the scene some extra detail or a new ending.

In the space below, draw a picture of your house or dog or backpack, but do it all wrong. Make every color different.

Alternate Nostril Breathing

Sit up tall and,

using your right hand,

close off your right nostril with your thumb as you inhale slowly through the left nostril.

Then, close off your left nostril with your ring finger,

and exhale slowly through the right.

Then, inhale slowly through the right,

switch fingers,

and exhale slowly through the left.

Repeat this for five minutes.

Pretend right now that
this moment is exactly
as you chose it to be.
Close your eyes and
savor the moment.

Whenever possible, all day today, write with your non-dominant hand.

What is the best advice you have ever received from a teacher or minister? Write it below.

Do something unexpected three times today. You can wear a bright pink shirt, buy a friend coffee, sing in public, skip down the street, be selfish or selfless, give up the perfect parking spot, tell a joke, dance in the rain, anything unexpected.

Record your three unexpected actions below:

1. ______________________________

2. ______________________________

3. ______________________________

Sometimes you break a rut not by changing your habits and doing something new, but by appreciating what you already have. In the space below, list fifty awesome things about your life.

1. ______
2. ______
3. ______
4. ______
5. ______
6. ______
7. ______
8. ______
9. ______
10. ______
11. ______
12. ______
13. ______
14. ______
15. ______
16. ______
17. ______
18. ______
19. ______
20. ______
21. ______
22. ______
23. ______
24. ______
25. ______
26. ______
27. ______
28. ______
29. ______
30. ______
31. ______
32. ______
33. ______
34. ______
35. ______
36. ______
37. ______
38. ______
39. ______
40. ______
41. ______
42. ______
43. ______
44. ______
45. ______
46. ______
47. ______
48. ______
49. ______
50. ______

What are your three best jokes? Write them here.

(Note: If you don't have three best jokes, time for some research.)

1. ______________________________

____

____

2. ______________________________

____

____

3. ______________________________

____

____

Do something every day this week that makes you laugh. This can include lunch with an amusing friend, watching a hilarious YouTube clip, reading comics, or watching puppies play in the park. Keep track here:

- ☐ Monday: ______________________________
- ☐ Tuesday: ______________________________
- ☐ Wednesday: ______________________________
- ☐ Thursday: ______________________________
- ☐ Friday: ______________________________
- ☐ Saturday: ______________________________
- ☐ Sunday: ______________________________

Write a poem or short song here. Act like you are a poetic genius. You are Jim Morrison, Bob Dylan, and Joni Mitchell. Even if just for right now, be completely confident, even arrogant. Believe that you have just created a culturally important masterpiece.

Write a mini-memoir on this page. Write one sentence that goes with each year or decade of your life.

What do you want the next chapter to tell?

Take one small action today to set that into motion.

Cut out and paste or draw a picture of a famous painting here.

Then, add to it. Make it better, or at least different.

Watch for the next time you feel resentful. What are you resenting? What can you do to feel that you have a say in the situation? What can you do in the situation to feel more empowered?

List five of your personal strengths. Be honest.

1. ______________________________

2. ______________________________

3. ______________________________

4. ______________________________

5. ______________________________

Does your work harness your strengths?

(Secret fact: It's okay to choose work that harnesses your strengths).

Mindfulness 101

All day today, as you go about your work and chores and play, be present. Say, for example, "I am taking out the trash" as you take out the trash, and "I feel my feet on the ground as I walk to work, as you walk to work" and "I am typing a memo" as you type a memo.

Notice what this does for your mood, attention span, and energy level.

In what ways are you not
sharing your true self
with the world?

Why?

Can you change that?
Take a small step today
to be more honest with
the world.

Mindfulness 201

You are more than your mind.
Take a moment right now and
notice that you are thinking.

Who is noticing your thoughts?
That is the true you.

Turbo Rut Removal

Every time someone asks you a question, pause before you answer, and silently ask yourself *How do I really feel? What do I really think?* Respond to them as honestly as feels safe and appropriate.

Collect leaves today. How many different shapes and colors can you find? Press them here for a few days. Then, create art with them.

Close this book and do the most unlikely thing.

Write a secret here. Something you hold on to and have rarely (maybe never) shared with anyone. Maybe something you are ashamed of or something that terrorizes you.

Good. That was very brave. Now, tear out this page. You can burn it, shred it, bury it, or drive to the desert and leave it in the sand. Release it. Release the hurt. Release the shame. Release the pain. Release your guilt or terror. Start fresh, renewed.

III.

Heart

Free your heart and your spirit will fly free.

Express your feelings. Laugh. Giggle. Sing. Skip. Smile. Cry. Weep. Grieve. Yell. Infuriate people. Apologize. Make amends. Respect others. Appreciate. Love. Whisper. Shout. Be available. Be open. Be vulnerable. Be honest. Have gratitude. Be alive.

All great creativity

and aliveness

spring forth

from

an open heart.

Make connections in your local community and in your daily routines. Introduce yourself to your mail carrier and your garbage removal or supermarket check-out folks. Get to know your barista. Meet your librarian or hardware store clerks. Introduce yourself to your neighbors and have them over for coffee, a barbeque, or just a chat in the yard.

Make a list of beloved friends and relatives you have fallen out of regular touch with.

____

____

____

____

____

____

Program time into your calendar every Monday evening to call someone on the list.

Plan more social time than usual this week. Set up walks in the morning, lunches, dinners, movie night, roller skating, bowling, or a book group. Go to a yoga or spin class. Go out dancing or singing. Play bridge, chess, or bingo. Attend a talk at your local natural foods store, bookstore, church, temple, or library.

Notice which activities make you feel most alive. Do more of those.

With whom do you feel safe and free to express what you really feel and who you really are?

Make plans to spend more time with that person. Schedule a weekly lunch, walk, or phone date.

You deserve to feel robustly healthy and to enjoy your life.

(Circle one:)

Agree

Disagree

Now, what are you going to do about it?

Make a pilgrimage. Choose a teacher, minister, babysitter, or mentor who made a difference for you. Look them up and plan a visit.

Make a date with a friend to frolic. Meet in a park, take off your socks and shoes, and toss a Frisbee or jump rope. Just make sure it's fun and hopefully leaves you laughing.

Light a candle. Close your eyes. Steady your breathing, allow your mind to settle and relax, and then ask, "Why am I stuck?" Listen for an answer. It might surprise you.

Take notes here: ______________________________

____

____

____

____

____

____

What do you really want to accomplish in life? Write your answer below.

For the rest of today,
pursue what brings
you great joy.

Identify a trusty possession that is old and used up. Maybe your work bag, your coffee mug, your smartphone case, your ratty sweater, or your broken umbrella. Treat yourself to a new one today. Pick out a new one that makes you smile.

Clear the air. With whom do you have unsaid apologies?

Pick up the phone and say them now.

Who helped take care of you when you were little? Are you still in touch? Reconnect.

Who do you need to forgive and why?

Close this book, close your eyes, and meditate on forgiveness. Then, if it seems safe and appropriate, reach out via text or a phone call to someone you need to forgive.

When you were a kid, who made you feel safe and loved and appreciated?

Visualize that person appreciating your writing, painting, artwork, schoolwork, or business output right now.

Unstuck 101

Drop perfectionism.

(Even if for now you need to fake it.)

What would it take for you to be happy?

Is that your plan or someone else's plan for you that you've taken on?

Do you still agree with it?

What do you want more of in your life: money, free time, time to pursue your art or new business idea, love, passion, exercise, play? Find a few magazines and clip out pictures that demonstrate what you are seeking. Cover the rest of this page in a collage.

In a rut, it's easy to see other people, even those who are trying to help, as enemies, annoyances, or impediments. Instead, try to see everyone as an ally, a helper. Remind yourself throughout the day:

"Everyone is my ally, trying to help me in every way."

Watch how your interactions change when you change your perspective.

What is emerging in your life? What new energies/activities/life's work is attempting to emerge from you? What small simple step can you take today to encourage and facilitate its emergence?

Schedule a time this week to cook a fancy healthy dinner for someone you love. Maybe on a weekend when you won't have to rush. Take your time. Enjoy the process.

Place your hand on your heart. Close your eyes. Give a half smile and hum, like the sound you make when savoring something delicious. Purr like a cat. Do this for at least twenty seconds.

Afterward, notice how you feel.

Is there a piece of yourself you hide from the world?

In some way that feels safe, show at least some of that part today. This is like exercising a muscle to make it stronger; with practice you get better at sharing more of your true self with the world. And there is nothing more energizing and inspiring and rut-breaking than being your true self in the world.

Remember what it's like to be a kid today. Remember how free it feels. Kids laugh, and cry, and get in fights, and make up. They play. Find some way today in which you can be a kid.

Fill this page with your sadness. Every inch of it, till you can scarcely see any white space on the page at all. Get it all out. Then, tear out the page, lovingly crumple it up or shred it, and release your sadness into nature. Bury it in the woods, send it down a river, or ceremoniously burn it. It is time for a fresh start.

IV.

Spirit

You are not alone.

Feel God,

Your Ancestors,

Angels.

Let them in.

You are loved.

Let down your guard and feel connection,

feel love,

feel GRACE.

Write your name here:

____

(Color around it. Decorate it. Make it beautiful.)

Say your name aloud. Who are you, truly? Don't think. Just write.

Fill all the lines below.

After you read this paragraph, close your eyes and ask for a guide. This might be a beloved grandparent, a spiritual teacher, or a saint. Try it now.

Write the name of your guide here.

____

Ask for their help anytime you feel stuck.

This week, every morning, as soon as you wake up, say,

"love,"

"God,"

or

"peace"

first thing.

Creativity Baptism

1. Find a stream.
2. Take off your shoes and socks, roll up your pants, and step in.
3. Let the cool water wash away your fears, worries, and creative blocks.
4. Call upon God, your personal saints or angels, or Mother Nature for fresh inspiration.
5. Be refreshed and renewed.

For the rest of this week, go to bed an hour earlier and wake up an hour earlier. In the morning, light a candle and use the time in the morning to write, paint, do yoga, pray, or watch the sun rise. Leave this book on your bedside table so you'll remember.

Grab some colored pencils and use the bottom of this page to write "I surrender to the divine plan."

When do you feel most down and depressed and depleted? What places, events, or relationships?

You probably can't avoid those situations, but you can bring along help. Next time you are heading there, tuck into your bag the Bible, Yoga Sutras, Koran, a photo of your grandpa, or even your favorite novel. Reach for it and touch it whenever you need support.

Tomorrow, practice victory hands (arms up in the air, like "TOUCHDOWN!") for two minutes in the morning, at lunchtime, and at night before bed. Watch for miracles.

Don't be afraid of good things.

Repeat this mantra fifteen times:

"I claim my abundance from the universal account."

To whom have you given away power?

Take it back today. Imagine a subtle but strong boundary to your energy field. And in the center, near your heart, visualize a bright burning light, like the sun, shining and fueling you and burning out the pain and hurt and violation.

You are whole. Fully inhabit your body.

Today when you face a difficult or confusing decision, call upon a role model and ask,

"What would Jesus do?"

"What would Buddha do?"

Then, be brave and take action.

Paste a gorgeous photo of yourself below. Look at it anytime you doubt yourself and say aloud, "Look at you, you gorgeous, glorious beast! You are awesome!" (You have to mean it. No sarcasm.)

"If lovin' the lord is wrong,
I don't want to be right!"

—Reverend Brown in *Coming to America*

Agree or Disagree? Journal below.

Plan half a day or even a whole day this month to spend in silence.

Your own personal retreat. Just for the day, pretend you are a monk: eat simply, pray or meditate, walk mindfully, spend time in nature.

Choose a date: ______________________________

Schedule the day into your planner.

Record results on next page.

Every morning this week, right after you brush your teeth or shower, state this affirmation three times into the mirror:

"I express my gift in the world."

Perform a ceremony tomorrow morning. To prepare, eat simply today and go to bed early. Then, in the morning, light a candle and pray or meditate. Ask for guidance. What do you receive?

What would you do differently today if you had only a year to live?

Take the day off today and live it up.

Choose three times in your day to pause and appreciate something awesome in your life. Perhaps upon waking, before each meal, and at bed. At these moments, stop what you are doing, and state "My life is awesome because ___________________."

At the end of each of the next few days, record your three awesome observations here:

1. ____

2. ____

3. ____

About the Author

Brian Leaf is the author of fifteen books, including *The Teacher Appears* and *Misadventures of a Garden State Yogi*. Brian graduated from the Georgetown University in 1993 with a BA in business, English, and theology, and in 1999 he completed a master's degree at Lesley College, specializing in yoga and Ayurveda. He leads mindfulness, yoga, and productivity programs at businesses and yoga centers around the country. And, yes, he would love to keynote your annual meeting or event. Brian lives in Northampton, Massachusetts, with his wife and his two sons. Learn more or reach out to him at www.teacherappears.net.

Acknowledgments

Thank you, thank you to the many inspirations in my life: to Matthew Oestreicher and the Society for Free Living; to Eric Friedland-Kays; to Neal Jameson, Ross Bell, and Jeff Kalman; to Valerie Reiss and Sulis Sunrise Sophia; to Mike Brezsnyak; to Jean Zimmer; to Matthew Andrews; to X9 Games, Off the Wall Games, and the best game of all, Magic: the Gathering; to Nicole Mele and the whole Skyhorse team—you made this a better book and helped it meet the world; to Julie, Larry, Susan and Manny Leaf; and most of all, to Gwen, Benji, Noah, Neko, and Swami Kripalu.